Little Mitchie

SPIDERS THAT SPIN GOLD

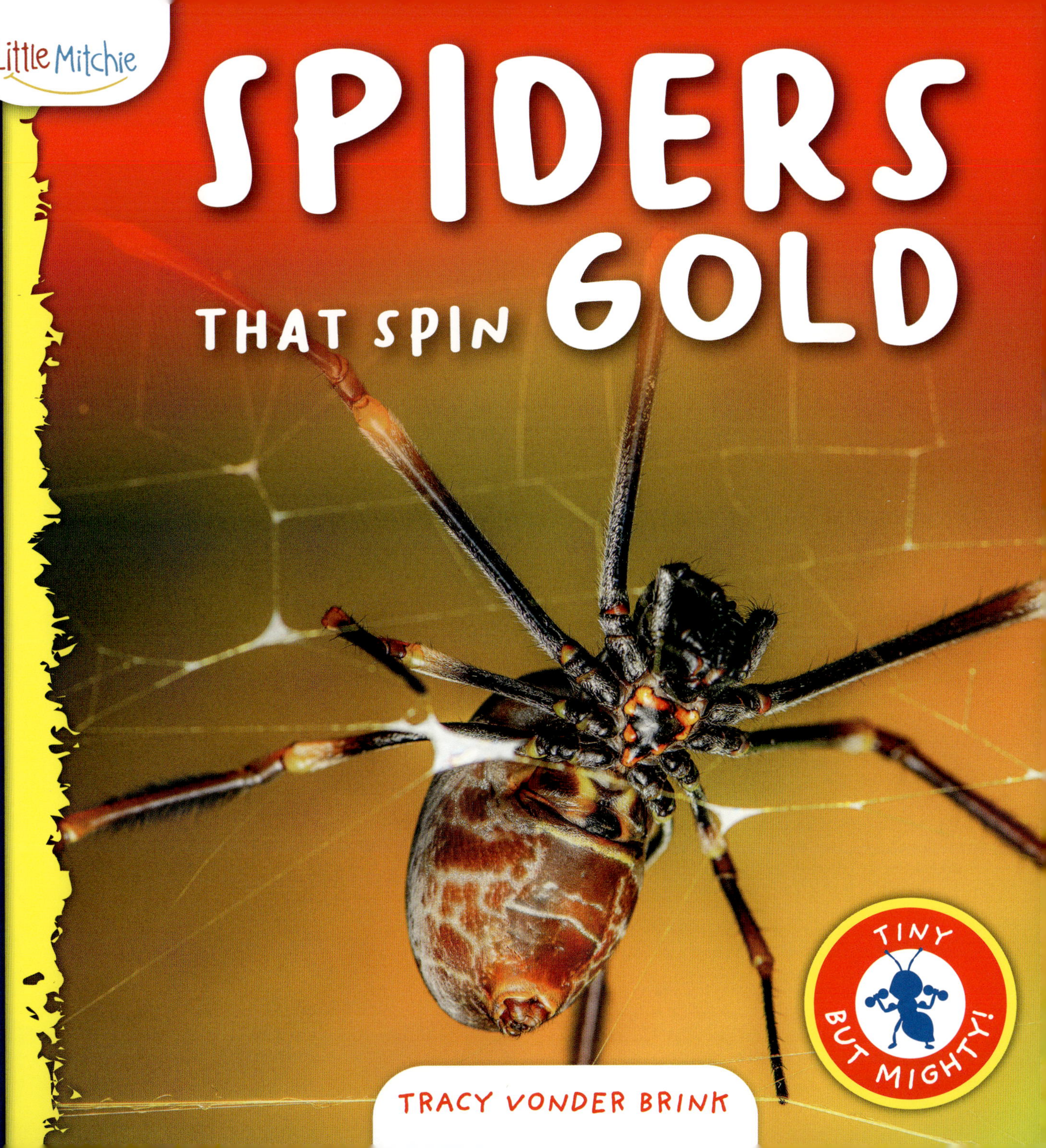

TRACY VONDER BRINK

CREATING YOUNG NONFICTION READERS

Little Mitchie books spark curiosity and support early nonfiction reading for students in Grades 2-3. Designed to build vocabulary, support second language learners, and prepare readers for middle-grade content, each book includes helpful tips for parents and educators to build confidence and deepen understanding of the world.

TIPS FOR READING NONFICTION WITH BEGINNING READERS

Talk about Nonfiction

Begin by explaining that nonfiction books give us information that is true. The book will be organized around a specific topic or idea, and we may learn new facts through reading.

Look at the Parts

Most nonfiction books have helpful features. Our *Little Mitchie* titles include color photographs and graphic aids, a table of contents, a glossary, and an index. Share the purpose of these features with your reader.

Color Photos and Graphic Aids

A lot of information can be found by "reading" photos, charts, maps, and other graphic aids found within nonfiction texts. Help your reader learn more about the different ways information can be displayed.

Table of Contents

Located at the front of the book, this list shows the big ideas within the text and the page numbers where they can be found.

Glossary

Located at the back of the book, the glossary defines key words and phrases that are related to the topic. These words and phrases can be found in the text in colored type.

Index

Located at the back of the book, an index is an alphabetical list of topics and the page numbers where they can be found.

With a little help and guidance about reading nonfiction, you can feel good about introducing a young reader to the world of *Little Mitchie* nonfiction books.

Little Mitchie is an imprint of:

Mitchell Lane
PUBLISHERS

2001 SW 31st Avenue
Hallandale, FL 33009
mitchelllanepub.com

First Edition, 2027.

Author: Tracy Vonder Brink
Designer: Jen Bowers
Editor: Tricia Hoffman

Library of Congress Cataloging-in-Publication Data
Title: Spiders That Spin Gold / by Tracy Vonder Brink

Description: Hallandale, FL :
Mitchell Lane Publishers, [2027]

Identifiers:
ISBN 979-8-89260-888-6 (library bound)
ISBN 979-8-89260-991-3 (eBook)

Library of Congress Control Number: 2026936361

PHOTO CREDITS
Shutterstock: cover, p.1 ©2026 Photography by Rob D, p.5 ©2012 FloridaStock, p.6 ©2012 Dustie, p.9, 22 ©2014 mycteria, p.10–11 ©2016 NeagoneFo, p.12, 22 ©2006 Liv Falvey, p.15 ©2018 Aris Suwanmalee G, p.16 ©2018 0 Lorenzo Bernini 0, p.17 ©2022 Komodo Studios, p.18, 22 ©2025 Auouououiii, p.21 ©2016 rzoze19, CC BY-SA 4.0/Matthew X Bird/Wikipedia

TABLE OF CONTENTS

Chapter One

A GOLDEN WEB

A spider's web stretches between two trees. It shines like gold in the sun.

MIGHTY MOMENT

Golden orb weavers are found in warm places around the world, including in the southeastern United States. They live in areas with trees and bushes.

Orb weavers are spiders. They make webs shaped like wagon wheels. A golden orb weaver is a kind of orb weaver spider. Its webs look like they're made of gold.

Chapter Two

MAKING A WEB

All spiders spin their webs with **silk** made inside their bodies. It comes out through **spinnerets**. Web-building spiders pull pieces of silk from the spinnerets. They make webs by connecting the pieces together.

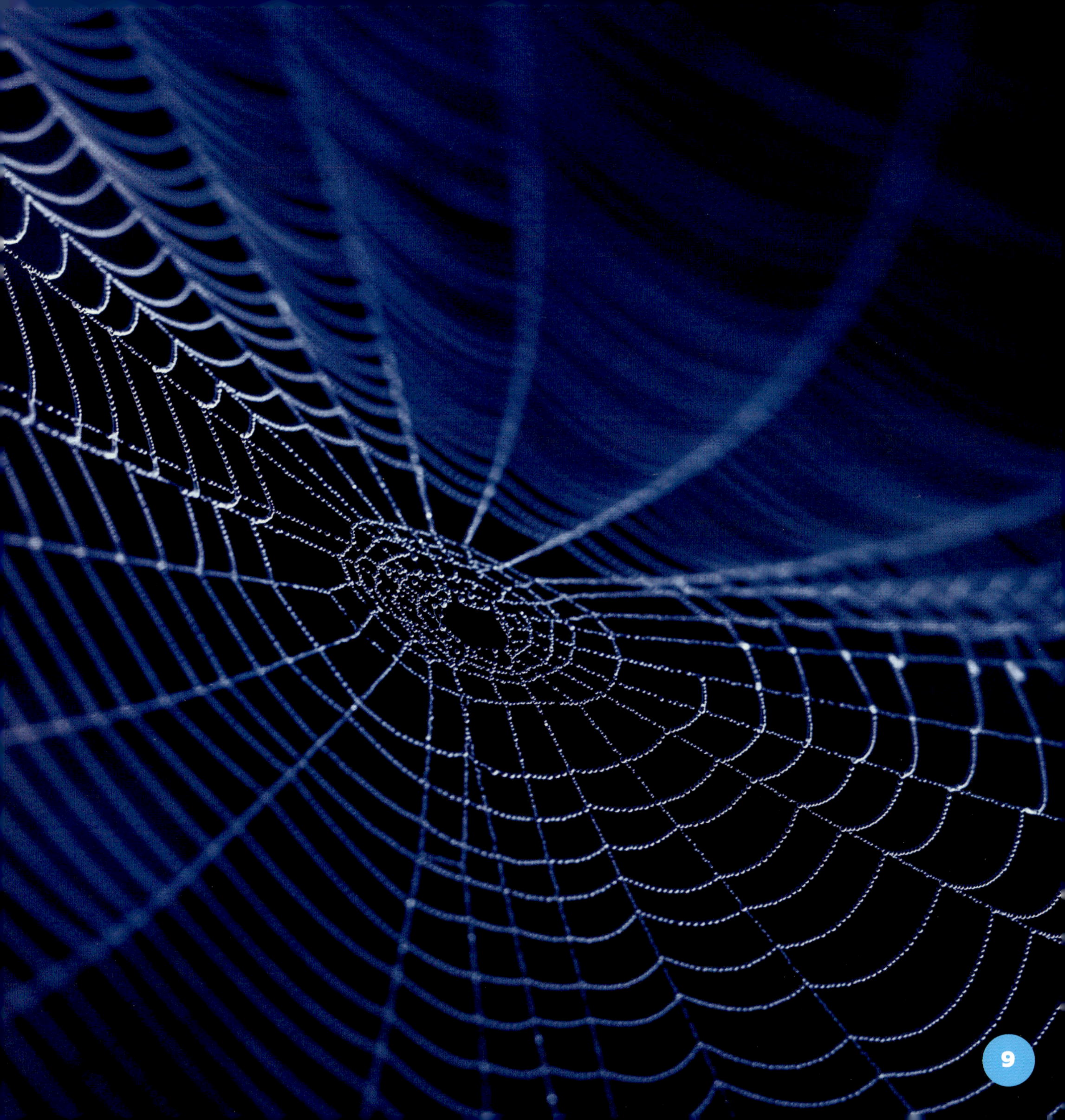

Spiders make up to seven kinds of silk. One kind is made to catch prey. Another kind is used to wrap up a meal. Some silk is used to **anchor** webs to things, like trees, and another kind holds spider eggs. Golden orb weavers make all seven kinds of silk.

MIGHTY MOMENT

Spiders don't get stuck in their own webs. They know which parts are sticky and don't walk there.

MIGHTY MOMENT

Male orb weavers are much smaller than females and don't spin webs. A male lives on the edge of a female's web.

Many orb weavers take their webs down every day and make new ones. But golden orb weavers leave the same web up day and night. Their webs are stronger than most spiders' webs. They can also fix any **damage** to the web.

Chapter Three

GOOD AS GOLD

Orb weavers' silk is often white. But golden orb weavers' bodies add **pigments** to their silk that make it look like gold. Why?

The gold color tricks bees and other insects. They think it might be a yellow flower and fly into the web. Instead of finding a flower, they become the spider's meal.

MIGHTY MOMENT

Golden orb weavers' webs can be up to three feet (1 m) across. They catch flying insects and sometimes even small birds and bats.

The color is also **camouflage**. It helps the web blend in with nearby plants. A hidden web keeps predators from finding the spider. Prey also can't spot it as easily.

Chapter Four

SPECIAL SPIDERS

Golden orb weavers make webs like no other spiders. The beautiful color attracts prey and keeps the spider safe. Their webs are amazing!

MIGHTY MOMENT

A team of craftspeople in Madagascar used silk from more than one million golden orb weavers to make a shawl and cape. It was shown at London's Victoria and Albert Museum in 2012.

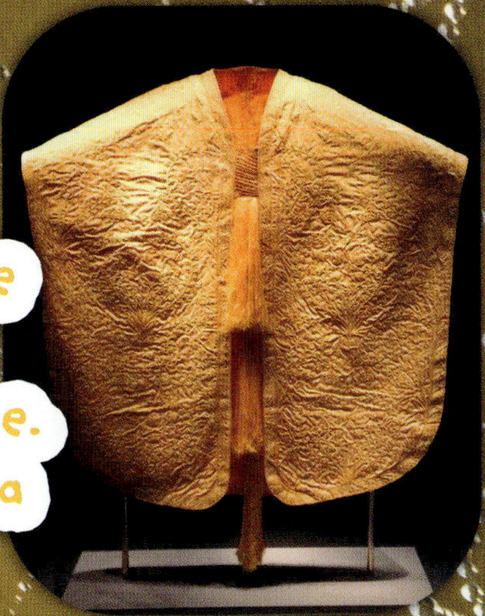

A CLOSER LOOK

Golden orb weavers can shake their webs to chase away predators. Other kinds of orb weavers do this too.

There are at least 50,000 kinds of spiders around the world. About half make webs to catch prey.

Male golden orb weavers are a different color than females. The tiny males have reddish-brown bodies.

GLOSSARY

anchor (ang-kur) to make something stay in place by attaching firmly

camouflage (kam-uh-flahzh) a way of making something hard to see by having a color or pattern similar to something around it

damage (dam-ij) harmed or broken in some way

pigments (pig-muhnts) substances that give something color

silk (silk) a material made by spiders and used in their webs

spinnerets (spin-uh-rets) body parts of spiders that produce threads of silk

FURTHER READING

Beccaloni, Jan. *The Secret World of Spiderwebs.* Thames & Hudson, 2025.

Howard, Tait. *Spiders: Worldwide Webs.* First Second, 2021.

ON THE INTERNET

Golden Orb Weaver

https://sdzwildlifeexplorers.org/animals/golden-orb-weaver

San Diego Zoo Wildlife Explorers is full of facts about the golden orb weaver.

Golden Orb Weaver Spider: Creature Power

https://pbskids.org/videos/watch/golden-orb-weaver-spider-creature-power/25196

This PBS Kids' *Wild Kratts* video shows you how a golden orb weaver spins her web.

INDEX